AFTER THE HATCHING OVEN

T0247359

AFTER THE HATCHING OVEN

David Alexander

NIGHTWOOD EDITIONS

2018

Nightwood Editions
P.O. Box 1779
Gibsons, BC VON 1VO
Canada
www.nightwoodeditions.com

EDITOR: Carleton Wilson
COVER DESIGN & TYPOGRAPHY: Carleton Wilson

Canada

Canada Council   Conseil des Arts
for the Arts   du Canada

BRITISH COLUMBIA
ARTS COUNCIL
An agency of the Province of British Columbia

Nightwood Editions acknowledges financial support from the Government of Canada and the Canada Council for the Arts, and from the Province of British Columbia through the British Columbia Arts Council and the Book Publisher's Tax Credit.

This book has been produced on 100% post-consumer recycled, ancient-forest-free paper, processed chlorine-free and printed with vegetable-based dyes.

Printed and bound in Canada.

CIP data available from Library and Archives Canada.

ISBN 978-0-88971-342-0

Contents

RUTA GRAVEOLENS

Man, when he is re-born, passes through the ages as he who is born; and the preceding state is always as an egg in respect to the subsequent one, thus he is continually conceived and born; and this not only when he lives in the world, but also when he comes into another life to eternity: and still he cannot be further perfected, than to be as an egg to those things which remain to be manifested, which are indefinite.

– Emanuel Swedenborg, *Heavenly Arcana Vol. VI*

The little face lifted on the long brown throat
sags, it widens, grows lips and eyelids,
whiskers, fleshy spines, warts and spangles.
New bones, new colors open in its skin,
new toes flex and take hold.
New claws, oh it scratches the itch on its back at last
and the back sprouts feathers, the feathers have feathers,
the feathers on feathers grow feathers; gladly intricate
and hard to see as anything living,
its infinite edges intimate with air…

– Sarah Lindsay, "Dinosaur to Dragon"

Rosmarinus Officinalis

Pray you, love, remember.

– Ophelia

Why Chickens Don't Fly

They never did rebel,
lacking a language
for revolution.

Seduced by cartoon myths,
content with minor
material improvements—

open windows,
bigger cages,
longer grazing periods.

The gene stamped out,
radical elements
rounded up:

docked,
debeaked,
culled to submission.

Upon understanding life is suffering
they ascend, Zenlike.

Κοτόσουπα

According to legend, Asclepius concocted
the first chicken soup to bring back the dead

son of Theseus. A still-beating heart
was quietly acquired from Alexis Carrel

when he died in 1944. This was added to a broth
made by Louis Pasteur, left to simmer for seventy years.

Patented by GlaxoSmithKline and fed to developing
embryos, the soup contained cholera. Thick with wattles

and gizzards and bones, the stew brought Hippolytus
back, but Asclepius was struck by a thunderbolt

for defying the old gods, furtive anti-vaxxers.
For best results heat on high for three minutes.

Review of the Royal Poultry House
from The Illustrated London News, 1843

In a secluded nook sheltered by stately elm trees
stands the private farm of Her Majesty. She seeks
the renovation of higher powers, which find their best

in homely recreations. The fowl house, designed and
built by Messrs. Bedborough and Jenner, is a semi-gothic
building. It consists of a centred pavilion crowned

by an elegant dovecote, and wings of symmetric
roosting houses and breeding nests. The ground in front
is enclosed and divided by light wire fences

for the run of the birds. Commendable regard to
the conveniences of their graminivorous tenants
has been displayed. The chambers spacious, airy,

warm. Their nests resemble the dark bramble recesses
of their jungles, twigs of heather and bramblets
of hawthorn covered over with white lichen.

The feeder of this family demands a passing
notice. Vigilant guardian protecting them
from enemies. Constant friend supplying

every necessity. And in due accordance with
gallinaceous law, adjudicating their disputes.

The Minimal Standing of Merely Conscious Entities

a cento from Why Did the Chicken Cross the World?

The gentleman keeps his distance from the kitchen
with wings that flap away the night. Don't try
to convey your enthusiasm.

The cock is like the souls of the just:
low cost and quick to reproduce the meta-
morphosis of the backyard bird.

He keeps the animal for its crow,
created to oppose demons and sorcerers.
Everyone else has to get up and go to work.

If you travel by railway, poultry becomes the subject,
like Mr. Perkins' steam gun, the intelligence
to distinguish between night and day.

Women carry them on their backs and raise
them as children not allowed to hatch because of
ethical guidelines drawn from the forest.

Pay homage to an animal,
the coming of the sun.

Genetic Extinction by Introgression

after ornithologist William Beebe

Researchers eat a chicken a night
in the sandstone hills of southern Jordan
discarding bones at site's edge.

An untameable leopard
no hint of the weak muscles
of the barnyard degenerate.

They seek proof of global travel
in old bones—hard enough to tell
the red from quail or francolin.

Low-hung tail, slightly bent legs,
head low, always intent, listening,
watching; almost never motionless.

It was discovered that Indus kept birds
in cages, but no one can say when
the fowl was domesticated.

Recognized as something alien, perhaps
superior, they took no liberties with him.

Reasons Farm Fowl Don't Take to the Air, Usually Employing Wings

They do not obey or carry out at any time,
do not have systems of words for communication,
for drastic action or change, often in politics.

Tempt, ensnare, entice by means of funny drawings, often
with dialogue or caption. Fictitious stories, often ancient. Happy
and agreeable to accompany tiny, tangible, bodily betterings.

Unfastened, honest, accessible framework with pane. Larger,
more generous enclosures with bars. Extended time to
touch or feed. Determiner DNA stepped on hard, gone.

A fundamental deviating by extremes. Basic essential features
driven together: cut short, remove the upper beak, pick out
for reason to force compliance. Fashionable comprehension.

Existence happens. Pain and agony. They rise,
resembling Zen Buddhism or some aspect of it.

Eating Wings

I wanted wings one night so I ordered six from some bright,
tiled place. I chewed through spicy tendons and veins
and dropped bones on the rain-kissed sidewalk.

Drawing Chickens
after Kate Sutherland

After tracing the head and upper plumage, move from
beak to thigh, sketching underbelly. The knife is plain
with a yellow plastic hilt. If male, exaggerate chest.

Or begin with an egg, tipped. Cracked where light gets in.
A beak will beat through, chick emerge headfirst, damp.
A wing, then legs dance free. If male, discard immediately.

Distinguish from duck and dove. Draw the beak and a long
metal box with a dial at the top. Turn the dial. Redraw beak,
rescinded. Fat-lipped. Knit its likeness a tea cozy.

Cast in iron on rooftops for a whirlwind spin or begin
by dabbing oil across featherless flesh. Picture the bird
in long grass. Render fat in boiling water.

Reduce 'til skin crisps. Embellish tail feathers.
Wattle and comb. A cage that resembles a kennel
crate. Repeat until chickens fill every inch,

shelved like paint cans. Dot a singular eye. Wings
etched at their sides. The beginnings of talons.

Why I Am Not a Chicken

after Frank O'Hara

I am not a chicken, I am a poet.
Why? I think I would rather be
a chicken, but I am not. Well,

for instance, Jo-Anne McArthur
goes into a factory farm.
It has CHICKENS in it.

"I want to liberate the chickens,"
I tell her. "The other animals, too."
I've never been inside. The days go by

and one day at a protest I see Jo-Anne's
photos. I write a line about chickens.
Pretty soon it is a whole page of words,

not lines. Then another page.
There should be so much more,
not of chickens, of words,

of how terrible slaughterhouses are
and life. My poem is finished and
I haven't mentioned chickens yet—

Divination of the Furcula

Chicken is a four thousand–year sociological phenomenon and agricultural unit that henpecks intrusive insects, eventually producing edible eggs and meat at a low cost. Its initial inputs are grains and water and sunlight and carbon and ideas about civilization. A chicken is unlike other birds. Adaptable to alien habitats and flavours. Willing to barter pain and death for species continuation, it thrives in jungles and ships and grasslands and islands and deserts and tundras and cages. Ancient pottery bearing a rooster's likeness was a vessel for the earliest known deep-fried drumsticks. The first chicken was born of gods who then ate that chicken and bore another and so on, etc. So sing the folklorists. The first chicken-egg problem, sing anthropologists. Charles Darwin solved his own chicken-egg problem by dissecting chickens and hoarding their skeletons.

A wishbone is a cruel joke.

Carbon dating established many delicious recipes. How to build a perfect coop. Set odds for a cockfight. Disconnect head from body. Studies suggest chickens experience intelligence beyond a pebble or clouds or celery. Canada's two official breeds are the Chantecler and the Avro Arrow. Invented by Oka cheese monks, the Chantecler is kin to American breeds but for its thick coat and gooey maple yolk. The Avro Arrow differs in that it is a decommissioned fighter jet. The Chicken of Tomorrow was a World War II research program like the Manhattan Project that, instead of weaponized energy, yielded a lucrative chicken progenitor. The only true heritage breed is red junglefowl. It bleeds indie cred. It cameos on *Portlandia*. It swaggers like Jagger in arthouse cafés. Surviving specimens are protected by a slaughterhouse owner on a hobby farm in southern Georgia.

He swears by their precognition. Some claim anarcho-communist sympathies. Without observation, nothing can be discredited.

Don't Flustrate, Take a Chillaxative

The elisionists never reblog,
lacking a laplet for revealalation.
Geophony drowns their sexting cakeholes,
but the lightbulb moment was sucktastic:
dodoed and dead-zoned, they cupcaked sustenance.
They arked it all, zerg-like. And so mysterians contend
with cultured meat—a national diet of rotisserated wingettes.

Chicken Cognition

They'll probably never read Jeremy Bentham
though his premise might ring.

And lack all understanding of ironic
timing, they won't open fancy cafés.

Not their station cybernetic modification,
leave burning chrome to cetaceans.

And unlike great apes, they won't paint great paintings,
won't click-clack the classics like monkeys.

They won't lead vast armies or start political
parties or script commodity fetishization.

Studies have shown that they do well in mazes
writing chicken scratch onto blank pages.

List of Fictional Chickens

Sheldon says he'd prefer not to hatch, he knows
where the bodies are buried. So Roy's the lone rooster,
a real Foghorn Leghorn. His job: protect hens from The Weasel.

The hens refuse to surrender their eggs. Little Red just wants
some goddamn baking assistance. Her plea goes out. Gyro Gearloose
builds a perfect oven, succumbs to it. Everything has a fatal flaw.

Far away, Billina hatches many Dorothys
and Boo fits in with Napoleon until the sky is falling.
Snowball won't be fooled. "He's a chicken, I tell you,"

he tells you, propelling their mutual downfall.
Camilla charms her beau, Gonzo, but doesn't know
he just loves *the idea* of loving a chicken.

Chicken Little cries. The hens smash their eggs. The Party
starves them. The Weasel waits for Alectryon to drift.

Chicken Behaviour and Welfare

after an online course

Feeding is controlled between brain and gut. So how can you limit cannibalism? Animals express eating and food-seeking over eight thousand years. Animals work even when they don't need to. Poultry start before a chicken. To live and be of use to humans is no reward or punishment. Chickens have panoramic vision, better red and orange. We see between flocks. A white cockerel might be ultraviolet. The broiler chicken is metabolic heat. Fracture is common. The tendency to perform harder for us. Comfort movements temporarily relieve tension. Waltzing, tail wagging, strutting, head shaking, bill wiping, preening. First you will see restlessness. They nest and nest and phase their inability to walk properly. Many matings are incomplete phases. Sham behaviour. They tend to land badly. So if you want hens you'll be losing revenue even if you don't get perches and adequate space. In a shed you have complete crates. People like to keep. It is easier. Behaviour is defined as the overt expression of what's going on. Depopulation takes place at night. Catching crews feel birds take advantage of food and water. Unfortunately chicks hatch male and don't grow to lay eggs so those need to be destroyed. Sadly pecking at droppings is escape behaviour. Check the bird. Another definition is a state of harmony. To reduce, pen hens on solid sand or whatever. There are various animal welfare organizations. At some time, you keep chickens old or perhaps sick or injured. There are several methods of destruction. Cervical dislocation would kill a small number, for example up to seventy birds per day. Never assume your killing has worked. A bird is dead? Birds often die. Some religions don't cut from the body. Sometimes reflexes make the bird dead if a bird shows it is very important. They're kept until their turn to go. Stunning stops them from suffering the actual dying process. Always check local regulations. Whatever happens, no one should kill an animal.

In the Fenced Back Patio at Dusk

Chickens haunt branches strung

with red and white lights. Phones trill.

Smoke streams. Tree wings bend

with birdsong's weight. As we sip

Red Roosters, a burly server plucks

a meaty lad by his hackles, corrals him

into the open kitchen. Its hatch slams shut

and no one is quite sure how it's done but

everyone's happy when the food arrives.

Across the Road

A chicken has reasons
for wanting the other side.

It's more complicated than a nursery rhyme
or a joke ending "Kentucky Fried."

"Why me?" she pled to the bluebird
and cried.

Bellis Perennis

She died.
The daisy petals tipped, then
blotched with red.

– Robin Skelton, "A Chain of Daisies"

Being Chicken

You hatch,
but before you hatch your
brothers and sisters are chirping

Your mother feeds you,
you are hungry from being
born, you feel you could live ten years

She shows you dust bathing
to clean your feathers and shake
off parasites

In communal flock
roosters cluck for you, tidbitting
beetles and seeds

You roost together for warmth,
home is the highest protected location

Avian Influenza

Beware of sneezing and runny eggs I mean
puffy eyes. I mean ruffled feathers and a drop
in egg production. Beware 90 percent mortality over

forty-eight hours. Depopulation of infected
flocks, quarantine of exposed flocks,
surveillance of nearby flocks are

preferred control methods. Outbreaks
concern us for several reasons: mutation of
viruses, rapid spread of illness and death

among poultry, impact of trade restrictions,
transmission to humans. Animals pose a threat
to human health. Do not handle

sick or dead poultry. If infected do not
give away your condition. Continue operating
heavy machines and motor vehicles.

Drive into the sunset. Drive to California.
Drive until it all breaks down.

Wing Menu

Mild
Wild, you hightailed when the hound wailed
at the full moon. Feathers sell, you uttered
from the other side. Your wing tapped.
You shook tight
into the night

Medium
Tedium, you sky-sailed when helium failed
the full moon. Feathers swell. You fluttered
to the other side. Your wing flapped.
You took flight
into the night

Hot
Fraught, you guys bailed when the shot sailed
into the full moon. Feathers yell. You sputtered
on the other side. Your wing slapped.
You hook right
into the night

Suicide
Blue inside, you cry,
nailed to a full moon. But you reside
in the other side. Cut feathers. Heat trapped. White.

Erasure of "The Hen"

after Ted Hughes

The dust god does not care. She
has forgotten cleavers, hot ovens,
the penknife blade splitting her wings

like empty sky. She rakes dirt, clucks
alarm instead of song. The Creator
separated her. The heavens have

fallen. And she is punished instantly.
She of nothing, except a slight,
closed sleep, the odour of—

Counting Chickens

At crosswalks they stand on shoulders,
three-to-a-trench-coat. One does cartoon voices.
One preens from a billboard above the library.

Six small chicks and their ma can't recall
the moral of this short time together. Curled up
on the couch, their snores sound like daisies.

They ride bikes and rent converted garages,
yet still we drive past them on trucks. Yet still
when they hatch, cuts of meat explode out.

Watch what they do when an egg won't stop
rolling. When they really go at each other,
cha-ching! Advertising.

Before hatching, amateur fortune tellers
often find themselves in personal banking.
Baking? You wish. Sharp suits dignify death.

Whispering wings in a backyard run.

Woman Returns Home, Finds Flying Chicken in Kitchen

Is there a colony of chickens in my attic?
A nest somewhere? Googles what type
of chicken, best ways to kill.

Looking at oven, frets. Did I leave
the chicken on? Leafs crisp yellow pages.
Still its wings beat. The question is not

can they suffer, but why they're such
a pain in my ass. Brief touchdown on
melamine. Nips breakfast crumbs, overturns

compost, scoops coffee grounds and
decaying kale. The chicken turns—
"So surprised to find I have my own desires?"

She drops to the floor. The doorbell rings.
What a beautiful bird, she remembers.

When God Discovered Chicken

after Ted Hughes

Her feathers are beach stones the colour
of autumn leaves. God does not want to look.
He cracks her shell and she erodes. Copper
pennies, weathered metal, brick.

He scratches. She lets out a puff of ash,
turns velveteen. He rubs until she sprouts
blank feathers and tugs—
now she's shrouded in white.

Chicken does not like to be white
so she plucks bare her legs,
peels the skin from her beak.
A red gash opens

over her head,
around her cheeks.

Let Them Be White

Like a bare unlined page. Like serviette
origami. Like a prom night limousine. Like melting
vanilla ice cream. Like stacks of clean T-shirts
and underwear. Like your aunt's dinnerware, her house
in Oshawa. Like hardboiled eggs. A ghost of
bedsheets. Chalk streaks on a blackboard. Clouds
against blue sky. Like an airplane or its contrail.
Like someone's idea of heaven. Like a thick coat
of primer in your first apartment. A kitchen catcher.
Disposable forks. Elmer's Glue. The flesh of Wonder
Bread. Like the pressed shirts of boys who sing for
their parents. A sharp intake of breath. Like you see
before fainting. Like a rabbit or snowy owl.
Like being struck by lightning. An arctic fox
or a dove. Being released from a dark cell.
Like Vicodin. Dust masks. Fluorescent
lights. An empty signboard. Dressing a wound.
Cooked meat. Teeth. Cooked meat. I've said that.

Translation, 1941

In Italy, *chicchirichí* was decreed
and no one was allowed to leave
the countryside.

Food rationing in Britain meant
everyone had to share their clucks
until they had none left for themselves.

It is a little-known fact that Orloff hens
infiltrated the Wehrmacht with their
melancholy songs of *ko-ko-ko*.

The Cornish were programmed to chirp Morse
and map gulags in dirt—*cock-a-doodle*
was code for "The Germans are coming!"

Piou piou is a French expression that
translates roughly to "A chicken dies
a thousand times."

If not for Leghorns, we'd all be speaking
kikeriki or *ku-ku-ku-ku*.

Song for the Gamecock

The small nation that achieves
victory over a larger one tells
and sings of it forever after.
  – José Rizal

The spur is a dagger,
you understand this.

Survive two and
you're famous.

Three, you'll retire
and sire new birds.

They come to wager,
to do what men do.

The fight will be over
in ninety seconds.

The Name Game

towards each other two drivers drive
one must swerve or both die

the loss in swerving is trivial
if one believes one's opponent
reasonable, one may decide not to

if one swerves and the other does not
the one who swerved will be called "chicken"

a chicken called the one who swerved
"does not the other swerve to

decide not to?" an unreasonable
opponent believes one's
trivial swerving is the loss

to die, both must swerve
drive each other towards each other

Habitat

The lights gleam / you could hardly sleep / through chirping and clawing / the birds push / for what feels like forever / the smell of ammonia overpowering / a vinyl shed the size of a garden centre / where a cockerel ekes out a place for himself / his knees ache / his mangled beak drops a seed / for one pullet in a sea of scarlet crests / as birds push for what feels like forever the lights gleam / the smell of ammonia / you could hardly sleep.

White Lies / White Meat

after "Two Legends" by Ted Hughes

White was the vision of the blind chicken,
white the feathered skin. White was the head.
White the neck, white the breast.

Lungs filled with light. White the blood
and the bird shit. White too the wings
that beat at the night. White the throat,

white the syrinx. The cluck's inflection,
its moonlit reticence. White the frail hymn
that crows for the sun.

White, the tail of the fox in the grass.
White, the truck transcending the highway.
White, the conveyor birds hang from.

The covered windows, white as
eggshells. Outside, the heavens
drift. To kill a chicken,

a veil of vapour rises
and cools. Then falls.

Programming Your Mind to Feel Positive
in the Company of Chickens

at my flesh with their claws
the mind flocks to that day
they saw threat for whatever reason

a violent streak
their talons, their beaks
from those beady unblinking eyes
they coordinate their attacks
at my eyes every time a friend
brings up free range eggs

deformed Werner Herzog
made this noise that chilled me
unaware chickens trigger
nausea, shaking, heart palpitations
irrational I freaked
counselling and medication
conquering one by one
many a good roast chicken

Cento for a Chicken with His Head Cut Off

The pan crackles and spits with fat
and eggs / anyone's egg will do, any egg /
signifying calm, resignation, oblivion /
and a future of empty sky / of clashing
cleavers, of hot ovens / Still your quick

tail and lie as dead / arms: you want
to savage the bird / who cuts his own
throat, who bleeds / his chicken song
way down in his throat, / his torn out,
bloodied feathers drift down / A hen

with wire under her feet, wire at
her beak, beak / beside the white /
touches the blade of his killing
knife / The sky is dark / with chickens, /
dense with them / She has forgotten

flight / the smell of chicken feed
overwhelms me

Dead Chickens

1. At a table set for two
   a candle tickles chicken
   with delicate yellow light.

2. *Dead Chicken*, etched ketchup red.
   The murder weapon gleamed
   like a sharpened pen.

3. Chickens hang—
   longing for the feathers
   of their silent wings.

4. Rollover, 401.
   Firefighters chase the quick
   through chicken smoke.

5. I know how the chicken lived
   and how the chicken died.
   I know nothing at all.

6. The barn. Aflame.
   Chickens. Aflame.
   A siren oscillates.

7. A dark cloud of dead chickens,
   risen. A great ape, agape.

Poulet de Bresse

A famine came and dried out all the rain. A cockerel
went afar in search of grub. He came across a fox
who tendered an emissary gift—to greet travellers

with a kiss. The cock crowed and leapt and waited
on a ridge until the fox grew hungry and darted off.
Next he came upon a cat. The cat said she was sent

to silence his bird blather and if he didn't shut up
with his crowing he'd be done. The rooster cawed
and crossed her. The cat caught sight of a field mouse

and fled in pursuit. He came to a pasture where
a golden hen was fed the finest corn and wheat and
whey and left to frolic, but strangers kept scheming

to cleave her open and claim her eggs. She vented.
They came upon caged siblings, crying,
with red and yellow hair. An ogre was found

in the farmhouse kitchen. He pushed him in an open
oven and it rained all day. The chanticleer crowed.

Animal Enterprise Terrorism Act

Rubber chickens fly through the enclosure
blowing cages and fire doors open.
Chickens rush the Ontario woodlands

and on TV a Ronald McDonald says
he's sorry for making them nuggets.
Why and to whom he's not sure,

but his makeup is running. Beads
of white sweat and red tears streak
his painted face. And perhaps

he was held sixteen weeks
in a basement and a pointed gun
just out of view holds a script

so now he's condemning America,
fast food, civilization. And maybe
a guy in a chicken suit left the gates

to the cattle ranch open, left the
ranchers there shot in cold blood.

Ruta Graveolens

Rue, not rage
Against that night
We go into,
Sets me straight
On what to do
Before I die—

– Samuel Menashe, "Rue"

Invisibility or Flight?

Think of it
as a kind of weightlessness.
To be hidden is a kind of leap.

Romans were first
to raise chickens indoors.
We were first to keep thousands.

Invented breeds yield
oversized breasts. Scientists
pilot humane enclosures.

They call one aviary. The birds
breathe dust and ammonia.
When flu comes

they literally melt. We call it open
air. Think of it as knowing
you're unable to fly,

that what goes up
can't be erased.

Study: Tyrannosaurus Rex Basically a Big Chicken

On the eighth day Tyrannosaurus was the most dangerous
creature around. He chased the other dinosaurs across
the Cretaceous but eventually grew so lonely he went

extinct. The link between chickens and ancient
theropods was revealed after we feasted on
Gallimimus wings at a great archaeological dig.

Rex was overthrown by tree-hopping feathered raptors
who must have been inside when the meteor struck
or the ice age came. Whatever. Reborn as Basilisk,

he survived the long night and by the time any of us
figured how to compose durable texts and images,
Basilisk begat the fearsome Junglefowl, destroyer

of bugs, who begat Rooster who called forth the day,
which used to be a big deal, and he was also considered
a sex god. But now he's just Chicken and even though

he sires fire-breathing chicks with long tails
and sharp claws, no one's afraid anymore.

Who Made Your Eggs Today?

after an Egg Farmers of Ontario ad campaign

Adam Bauer squeezed one out
this afternoon in Elgin, Ontario.
It's what he was born to do.

They don't mind rubbing elbows—
social animals find comfort
in small spaces.

Organic corn makes for a sweeter
final product. Happy farmers;
healthy eggs.

Four months until he's spent.
If not for agriculture,
they'd go extinct.

He's treated better than
most cats or dogs.

Undercover Investigators

The odds of being singled out as inhumane
are infinitesimal. Even the larger ones who
churn out thousands are rarely investigated.

Poems are stupid. Who's to say
what one wants? A poem doesn't know
it's a poem or make moral choices.

Have you heard of these people who infiltrate
our production lines? If it's as bad as they say,
how do they bear witnessing?

And if they discover neglect or cruelty,
they should stop right there
and inform their employer.

Poets aren't evil. We just write
for our own enjoyment.

Rooster Poem

One rooster always tells the truth,
one always lies. One grants fertility
and fortune, another dies. The world

was created when a cock sprang from
egg immaculate and ended when the last
true junglefowl had a panic attack.

What's left is lab meat, taxidermied pheasant.
Time was when roosters warned of this. If
they still do, only shaken farmhands linger.

If through their earplugs, goggles, protective
masks, they hear a bird call forth the sun
to shine a light, shine a light, shine a light

and all they do is blast the halogens,
something's lost. A rooster's fine
protection, a loyal augur—

not a mischievous bone in his body,
it's catalogued.

Incantation for a Chicken Nation

You who are in all of us yet speak in tongues—
You who exercise our incisors, who dissolve in our throats—
You whose clucks and chirps we have no ear for
though we find you on the tips of our tongues—

What elegies reside in the pink slabs of your flanks?
What aria froze in your stilled heart? You,
whose souls are deemed inaudible,
where do you sleep?

Elegy

Here she lies, unknown, at rest
on a bed of rue and rosemary. Tenderly

trussed before cremation. She loved your
jokes about bacon, the winking way

you hawked her hand-drawn corpse.
She gleamed at how she helped you

lose ten pounds. Her children trampled in
feedlot trenches that she might simmer

in your eulogy. Inscribed in air
above her unmarked grave:

Who was she? Was she
yours? A rooster cries.

Subservient Chicken

after a Burger King ad campaign

If they told you to hop on one foot
you would leap. If they told you
your leg was just meat you'd

be meat. If they said you were dumb
you would have to agree and if they said
your bird brain was a box you would not

cry and if they said you weren't even
a bird you would not fly. If your breast
was worth $6.99 you would not haggle

and if they told you how they liked it
you would be that way. If they asked,
"Can I eat you?" you would die

and if they told you to pray you would
flap your wings. If they said
to lay six eggs a week you'd lay

eight and if they asked you to rage
would you rattle your cage?

The People Eat Them and the Meat Is White and Tastes Like Chicken

A chicken is a message, / pink and
package ready. Its body, a springboard /
forgiving him, embracing him,

inviting / perhaps boiling chicken for supper; /
there is no smell to pain. / The chicken bleeds.
Even here the sun is crushed, / and Cheetos,

all organic grain-fed pieces of
chicken / dropped and found again. /
Who sounds loudest in my head / and swirls

the bird in circles, a fine / chicken
sandwich you ate afterwards. Ashes have
memories / of more. You are the most important

chicken in history, / tied and trussed,
drumsticks like punching bags, cooking /
tasty wizards / with such gusto it lifts

loneliness off. / The ghosts, if any,
clear / thus do I produce meat.

The Chicken Knows

Six summers caged at Smithfield
a lone survivor dons a mask
saves thousands from a barn fire

The papers call her "Pollo Libre"
tabloids howl "Fair or Fowl?"
teens write crossover anthems

Officers ponder her
corny crime scene one-liners—
cracked eggs and homes-to-roost

In the sheds
birds jostle tightly
floodlights blaze for eighteen hours

Now she leaps one
haunted and hollow
for impossible vengeance

There are things that happen in the light
and things that happen in the absence of light

Don't Have the Wings for It

Those fuckers. Those idiots prayed.

We killed their heroes: sexy bunnies and

blustery cocks, pleasure's victories awaiting…

And more money would be nice to house our

parakeets. And what do we mean by the standards

sand shift? And will we mechanize until all the outlaws

are their pistols? Like those fit for it—unwilling to submit to

keeping order restored—we went awry like free spirits, high as kites.

Locavorism

Everyone should lock eyes with
their food at least once. Everyone

should look a bird in the eye under
the hanging trowels and extension cords

of a DIY abattoir. We must each know
a man who kills. The knife's edge in

his eyes and how things die. A cloud's
low thunder. Come nightmares or gratitude

our feelings don't matter, but know
that I know what the dead do not.

And return me to earth
a sunbeam. A delicacy.

When the Sky Is Falling

A sparrow's serenade,
my perfect drug

Spring a cage, hop
a fence, pray sky-struck

Oh domed mural! Stratospheric,
dizzying oracle

To stumble is freefall
with muscles extended

If wings can catch, wind can
gasp, a spec of dust blind

What is up? What is
down? What is sky?

They Killed the Chickens

They killed the chickens they killed puddles and
threw our umbrella and ate the chickens and
one called the cops because sweet and soft and
innocent of fowl the clerks chased us stricken
from the final poem camping and could not
be signatures for a petition to save the library
which was going out of all the chickens killed
stopped working so we picked names like
Boo and Garage Sale and used them too
did I exaggerate when I said one hundred
and it started raining again
did I sound hysterical?

And It All Washed Out

After the rain we hopped the chickens they killed
and cooked a Tim Hortons window no chickens
previously so white and didn't trust police authority
and none play oh goodness they will just have to
call their manager who I am tempted to gather
reached. We hopped to the great memorial
for all the names because all the books
would have about a hundred billion some poems
out from their little and penny and business
did papier-mâché and then it billion
you'd think this whole thing
and it all washed out.

After bpNichol

A
cluck

A
click

A
chick

A
child

A
chill

Salvia Officinalis

Things do not change; we change.

– Henry David Thoreau, *Walden*

Can Chickens Love You?

It's time to stop hugging your chickens.
We know you love your chickens,
but please don't do this. Suspending

a chicken over your bed could protect
against Zika virus. Hundreds of chickens
on death row rehomed in a weekend

using Facebook. Georgia woman wrecks
chicken truck, says she's vegan. Thousands
of chickens escape on motorway and hop

into cars. Chatham County 4-H unites children,
chickens for Easter. Massachusetts retirees
knit tiny sweaters to warm backyard

chickens. All your favourite vacation spots
have been overrun by feral chickens.

Gonna Give It to Ya

after a KFC *ad campaign*

The chicken,
a domesticated
bird-like product

swaggers to DMX
no stuttering windup toy
no squeeze my foot to hear

The whole chicken, yours
like a sack of potatoes
glares down camera:

bobs head
tilts neck
dares personhood

And nothing but the chicken
no paper bucket on the table
no deep-fried disguise

dissembling her material conditions
ready to give

"Why chickens?"

asks Ben, who feels more kinship
with sheep, cows, pigs. So I tell him
because they sing such pretty songs,

because the slaughterhouse is not
a metaphor for something else,
because birds are often used

as stand-ins for poets, because
among land-based vertebrates
our most populous rivals are

the brown rat and Gallus gallus
which numbered 18.6 billion in 2009
according to FAO estimates

because I feed my cats chicken
because when people stop eating cute
pigs or red meat they switch to chicken

and more suffer and die
because each one is small

You Ate a Lot of That Weird Chicken

You'll soon run out of chickens, Louis. Hell,
I slept in the chicken coop a whole lot of nights.
Did I hear clucking? Did someone bring a chicken
in here? Why are you dressed like a chicken? Listen,

we either die free chickens or we die trying. Stickin'
feathers up your butt does not make you a chicken.
Remember, I can break your neck like
a chicken's. But you happened to pull this shit

while I'm in a transition period. The hard part about playing
chicken is knowing when to flinch. We'll show you
who's chicken! Watch this! (Harold clucks like
a chicken, then crows like a rooster.) He called you

a little piece of chicken. Do you remember when
you first came here, how you hated chickens? Well,
I've won over seven all-you-can-eat chicken wing

contests. I'm surrounded by man-eating chickens
right now. None of which you understand
because you are a chicken.

Aviary for Flightless Birds

First fill the sky with water. Let penguins swim
for fish and colonize horizon. Stub-winged
cormorants splash at clouds and perch

like silver statues on rocky, secluded islands.
Fuelled by flowers and figs, ostriches
streak vapour trails across open blue,

a flock of nomads fleeing fate—to be leather,
feathers, meat. Broadcasting from a floating
heathland, the mousey Atlantis rail patrol

a fern bush—secret entrance to their exile station.
Twilight beckons kiwi to root constellations
for grubs and hallelujah if they find some.

Chicken-sized, they fear chainsaws and stoats.
Sagittarius. Let the last kakapo *boom*
and *ching* and *skraark* his symphony

from a forest pit with newfound harmony.
Critically endangered like so many here,
his pleasant odour intones agreeable pet, but easy prey.

Parable of the Eagle

An eagle egg fell into a farmer's chicken shed
and when it hatched the farmer gave it chicken feed
even though he was the king of birds. The farmer

clipped the eaglet's princely beak and raised him
as a chicken. When he grew large, wildlife control
called on the farm. "It has the heart of an eagle,"

said the public servant. "It will fly." And the farmer
asked, "What if he likes it here with all the chickens?"
As they spoke, the birds crept off to don disguises.

Soon they couldn't tell the eagle from the hens
so they carried the strongest-looking bird to the
farmhouse balcony and said, "You're a regal eagle

not a lowly chicken. Go find your place in the sun!"
And they tossed one bird into the air together every
night until they fell in love, the farmer and the guy

from wildlife control, and got so hungry that they
ate roast eagle under a chicken-dotted sky.

American Standard of Perfection, 1910

from "Instructions to Judges"

The merit of specimens shall be determined
by a careful examination of all the points in
the "Scale of Points," beginning with symmetry

and continuing through the list, deducting from
the full value of each section for a perfect bird,
for such defects as are found in each specimen.

To receive a first prize the specimen must score
ninety or more points. Faking of any description shall
debar from competition specimens so treated.

In white varieties, except where plumage is specified
as creamy white, the presence of brassiness on
surface, or creaminess of quills or under-colour,

is a serious defect to be punished accordingly.
All score cards made out by judges applying
the standard are to be dated by the judge

with ink, indelible pencil, or by stamp
on the date the specimens are judged.

Chicken as Metaphor

i)

A cowardly idea
that goes down easy
can't regain flight.

Despite all the shit,
death and barbecue
sauce, a chicken

is just itself. Himself.
He cries before dawn
and you wake.

ii)

Songbirds sing. Mockingbirds, parrots,
these imposters draw praise. Sparrows
are bright and careless and these days

everyone's into falconry. Large birds of prey—
the eagle, the osprey—already crowd flags and
golf courses. In general, birds imply hawkishness.

Chicken seem hardly worth mentioning.
Ferocity, loyalty, wit…if these features are
relevant to your work, fowl make a poor choice.

A well-stationed rooster might serve on occasion,
but industrious writers favour wild pheasant
whose meek, spangled feathering

puts him in contention to be killed
by a fox or a hunting party. An owl's
something else altogether.

iii)

Kids love singing chickens
and pillowy pigs. Each creature
is key to all other creatures.

They don't mean what they sing.
Around the sun hurls the world.
We imagine a red barn, puffed with straw—

Blason de la Poule

her feet are two twig fingers grasping at grass
her legs support an ark that tips
like a theme-park ride, frequently stuck

her feathers are packed like fresh snow
her tail rises like an A300's vertical stabilizer
her chest puffs like a circus strongman's

her comb is a wavy cartoon mohawk
her wattle a red rubber mask
with hanging jowls

her wide open eyes have dust-brown irises
she jolts and tilts one
at you like this is an interrogation

her mouth is a broken duckbill
her No. 2 pencil-coloured underbite hangs
under slit nostrils and royal ridge nose

her wings flap like she's just realized gravity's threat
she flies a few metres but stumbles like a clumsy owl

Food of the Gods, a How-To Guide

> *He was suddenly taken with a vision of wildly growing chicks. He*
> *conceived a picture of coops and runs, outsize and still more outsize*
> *coops, and runs progressively larger.*
>   – H.G. Wells, *The Food of the Gods and How It Came to Earth*

First thing's containment. Erect coops large
as stadiums and high-fenced boulevard runs.
Populate with apple trees and giant slugs.

A suitable niche yields plentiful produce;
order new machines that butcher big,
and rounded forklifts for the giant eggs.

Colossal chicks hike workplace accident rates—
for your safety, mind the spur! Mangled limbs
and maulings haunt many an erstwhile amateur.

Unfit for titanic agriculture? Consider peril tourism.
Lost World Management for Dummies elucidates
effective adventure hunting sanctuary governance.

Use only as directed. Integrity suffers as mass
multiplies. Mammoth hens will collapse
at a yet-unknown magnitude.

We know six-times wings to be unflappable;
brief flight is thankfully unachievable.

Oculus Rift

Digital daisies lull chickens
/ dull wire-floor battery screams

Epic flight simulator for tethered breeds
/ we need 'til mass Petri meat flies

Let slip the surly bonds of earth
/ for a waking dream of red dirt

Footage from troubled Mars colony henhouse
/ disrupts duplicitous creeds

Of a transmission lost
/ screen dead as moonless sky

Phobos and Deimos plod by

Red Junglefowl

The range of the wild form stretches from
Tamil Nadu, South India, eastward across

southern China into Malaysia, the Philippines
and Indonesia. They are omnivorous and

feed on insects, seeds and fruits. Flight
is confined to reaching roosting areas at sunset

in trees or other high places relatively
safe from ground predators. The species

occupies tropical and subtropical habitats
including mangroves, scrubland and

plantations. It seems to prefer flat or
gently sloping terrain, forest edges

and secondary forest, or the foothills
of the Himalayas. The species owes

its decline to habitat loss and overhunting
for food. Its large range means it does not

approach the thresholds for "vulnerable"
under the range-size criterion. Although

the population is decreasing, the decline
is not sufficiently rapid to approach

the thresholds for "vulnerable" under
the population trend criterion.

Villanelle

we never fall or break apart completely our tears may
simmer as we float from crag to crag but we don't look
down so we never fall   the open air sustains us in 375°
heat   tears may simmer you may want us to scream
(and sometimes we do) but we never fall apart   wings
bend and flesh slips from our brittle bones (which you
snap)   tears simmer as we imagine looking down and
some of us drop but our tears never fall

After the Hatching Oven

A life is a set of physical properties
created or simulated under pretested
conditions. A life begins when an egg

is incubated for a certain amount of time
in appropriate heat and humidity with good
ventilation. A life begins in a closed universe.

A life begins when you push your way out.
A life goes on for a certain amount of time,
takes place indoors and ends too soon.

A life can be self-sustaining under certain
conditions for a certain amount of time in
a suitable synthetic environment. A life is

one of thousands in a world you cannot escape
or control. A life continues until it stops. A life
is a thing that has inherent value and ends

in the creation of value for someone else. A life
is over when the cycle ends, then repeats.

Massive Egg Cracks Open to Reveal Another
for Dennis Goslow

What came first—the egg large as an apple
discovered by a hobbyist in Echo Bay.
"They call me Egg Man now."

Heavier than a major league baseball,
a cloud breaks to reveal another,
he's not sure which hen laid it.

*

          At a nearby
       veterinary clinic
        an X-ray reveals
     (what can be known
        of such places) the
       ho-hum, egg-sized
             egg within

*

"I was a little sad. I had hoped
to eat it. If I live to be a hundred,
I'll never see that again."

*

Most kill their hens at two years old
when quality and output fall. "I can't.
They're my babies.

They get sick, I'll take care of them.
I've got two sleeping in my office
in a cage at night."

Notes and Acknowledgements

My thanks to the dear friends who provided feedback and encouragement on the poems in this manuscript. To Annick MacAskill, an excited and thoughtful first reader of many poems. To Stuart Ross for helping me hone my craft and experiment with new modes of writing. To Sue MacLeod for encouraging the egg of this idea. To Gretchen Primack, whose book *Kind* was a beacon on my journey to engage more deeply with animal issues. To Greg Smith for pointing me towards some great source material. And to my wife Stephanie for encouraging me to keep writing poems.

Thanks to Michael e. Casteels for publishing some of the early poems as *Chicken Scratch,* a chapbook from Puddles of Sky Press. Thanks to everyone at Nightwood Editions, especially my editor Carleton Wilson for strengthening these poems and helping to put everything in its right place.

"Aviary for Flightless Birds" appears in my chapbook *Modern Warfare* from Anstruther Press. "In the Fenced Back Patio at Dusk" appeared in *subTerrain.* "White Lies / White Meat," "Erasure of the Hen" and "Blason de la Poule" appeared in *Contemporary Verse 2.* "Food of the Gods, a How-To Guide" appeared in *The Puritan.* "Review of the Royal Poultry House," "Invisibility or Flight?" and "Red Junglefowl" appeared in *Hamilton Arts & Letters.* "The Name Game" appeared in *Bad Nudes.* "After the Hatching Oven" and "Why I Am Not a Chicken" appeared in the *Humber Literary Review.* "Drawing Chickens" appeared in the *Literary Review of Canada.* My thanks to the editors, staff and volunteers responsible for publishing and promoting my work and the fine work of many others.

The first epigraph is from a translation of Swedenborg's *Arcana Coelestia* published by Otis Clapp in 1843.

Several poems reference facts, sources and concepts explored in *Why Did the Chicken Cross the World?* by Andrew Lawler, especially: "Review of the Royal Poultry House," "The Minimal Standing of Merely Conscious Entities," "Genetic Extinction by Introgression," "Song for the Game Cock" and "American Standard of Perfection, 1910." Other poems started with ideas from Lawler's book and then I made stuff up; these include "Κοτόσουπα," "Divination of the Furcula," "Poulet de Bresse" and "Study: Tyrannosaurus Rex Basically a Giant Chicken."

The back slashes in the centos "Cento for a Chicken with His Head Cut Off" and "The People Eat Them and the Meat is White and Tastes Like Chicken" demarcate the specific lines taken from the various poems. The line breaks in the centos are my own.

The italicized lines in "Genetic Extinction by Introgression" are from William Beebe's description of the red junglefowl in *A Monograph of the Pheasants* (1916).

"Why I Am Not a Chicken" is after "Why I Am Not a Painter" by Frank O'Hara. Jo-Anne McArthur is an award-winning photojournalist, author and animal activist. Her work can be explored and supported at weanimals.org.

"Don't Flustrate, Take a Chillaxative" uses words found in the *Merriam-Webster Open Dictionary of New Words & Slang*.

"Chicken Behaviour and Welfare" is an erasure and remix of an online course from the University of Edinburgh.

"Avian Influenza" borrows language from the Centres for Disease Control and Prevention.

"Erasure of 'The Hen'" is an erasure of "The Hen" by Ted Hughes.

"When God Discovered Chicken" is in the style of Ted Hughes' *Crow*.

The last line of "Let Them Be White" is a riff on the poem "Fear" by Raymond Carver.

"The Name Game" uses and remixes text from the Wikipedia entry for the game chicken.

"White Lies / White Meat" rewrites the poem "Two Legends" by Ted Hughes.

"Programming Your Mind to Feel Positive in the Company of Chickens" is a remix of phrases found in the article "Alektorophobia: Fear of Chickens Is Surprisingly Common" from modernfarmer.com.

"Cento for a Chicken with His Head Cut Off" is composed of lines by Dani Couture, Sarah Lindsay, Robert Wrigley, Ted Hughes, D.H. Lawrence, Jennifer Michael Hecht, Charles Simic, Bruce Weigl, Elizabeth Bishop, Gretchen Primack, William Carlos Williams, Kay Ryan and Anne Waldman. It's not a true cento as it uses three successive lines—"The sky was / dark with chickens / dense with them"—from Kay Ryan's poem "Home to Roost."

"Dead Chickens" was inspired by Lillian Necakov's bird poems.

"Animal Enterprise Terrorism Act" is named for a US law that "sweepingly targets a wide range of political activity as 'terrorism' if done in the name of animal rights" (Will Potter, *Green Is the New Red: An Insider's Account of a Social Movement Under Siege*). Passed in 2006, the law prefigured many state "ag-gag" laws which have criminalized investigation of and whistleblowing against industrial animal agriculture operations.

"The People Eat Them and the Meat is White and Tastes Like Chicken" is a cento composed of lines by Robert Priest, Bren Simmers, Stuart Ross, Allen Ginsberg, Lillian Necakov, Sagawa Chika, Sina Queyras, A.K. Ramanujan, Edwin Brock, Bruce Weigl, Dina Del Bucchia and Daniel Zomparelli, Emily Schultz, Paul Vermeersch, Catriona Wright and Raoul Fernandes. The title, which refers to the meat of very large iguanas, is (erroneously?) attributed to Christopher Columbus.

"Can Chickens Love You?" is a composed of headlines from *Mother Nature Network*, *The Press Herald*, *Telegraph.co.uk*, ABC *Online*, *Associated Press*, *Savannah Morning News*, CBC.ca and *Atlas Obscura*.

"Why chickens?" is for my good friend Ben Kidd.

"You Ate a Lot of That Weird Chicken" is composed of lines from *Interview with the Vampire*, *The Thin Red Line*, *The Quick and the Dead*, *Home Alone*, *Chicken Run*, *Fight Club*, *Running Man*, *Pulp Fiction*, *The Hunt for Red October*, *Hook*, *True Grit*, *Taxi Driver*, *On Her Majesty's Secret Service*, *50 First Dates*, *Cloudy with a Chance of Meatballs* and *Moana*. The title is from *Bridesmaids*.

"Parable of the Eagle" is after a contemporary Christian parable.

"Chicken as Metaphor" uses the phrase "Each creature is key to all other creatures" from J. M. Coetzee's *Elizabeth Costello*.

"Red Junglefowl" uses found language from Wikipedia and the online *Encyclopedia of Life*.

"Massive Egg Cracks Open to Reveal Another" is for an Ontario man whose chicken laid an unusually large egg in 2017. I've borrowed heavily from Marina von Stackelberg's CBC News piece, including both her writing as well as her quotations of farmer Dennis Goslow. The title abbreviates CBC's headline for this piece.

About the Author

David Alexander is the author of the chapbooks *Chicken Scratch* (Puddles of Sky Press) and *Modern Warfare* (Anstruther Press). His work has been shortlisted for *The Walrus* Poetry Prize (2014), *Arc* Poem of the Year (2014), *FreeFall Magazine* Annual Poetry Contest (2016) and the Banff Centre Bliss Carman Poetry Award (2016). His poems have appeared in *Prairie Fire, The Malahat Review, Poetry is Dead, The Puritan, Humber Literary Review, subTerrain* and several other fine journals and magazines. David lives in Toronto and works in the nonprofit sector.

PHOTO CREDIT: CARLOS PINTO